Don't Let the Stock Market or I.R.S. Control Your Retirement!

Mark Kennedy

© 2016

Don't Let the Stock Market or I.R.S.
Control Your Retirement

© 2016 Mark Kennedy

ISBN: 978-0-9973228-0-4
1st Edition

Table of Contents

i

<u>Important Legal Disclosure</u>

Before I get into the 'meat and potatoes' of this book, the lawyers told me I had to share this page. We all love disclosures…but this is for your protection and understanding. So let's get this over with so you can read the most educational book in the country on retirement income planning!

First, there is nothing implied in this book that is 'guaranteed'. When I refer to 'guaranteed income' later on in this book, those guarantees are only as good as the companies that back them. It is important to know the strength of the companies you are dealing with.

Second, any rates of return stated or implied are 'hypothetical', meaning they are just examples. Nothing in this book is meant to make you believe that rate of return is solid or consistent or factual. Also, any tax discussions in this book are not meant as 'advice' and you should check with a competent licensed tax professional before proceeding.

Third, this book is from my viewpoint. Other advisors will have other viewpoints. Do not imply that anything that I write in this book is the only way to do something. Also, these strategies are not implied to work for everyone. If you do not stick to a budget or plan, the results will greatly differ.

Finally, there is a risk that you could lose all your money in the stock and bond market. Just because an account is 'conservative' doesn't mean it cannot have total risk of loss. The stock market and bond market both involve substantial risk and you need to be aware of that before investing any of your money.

All of the above being mentioned, let's get started!

Introduction

Why This Book?

Can you rely on the stock market for your retirement today? How will you keep up with future inflation and taxation? What is your plan to make sure you have income to last your lifetime?

I'm sitting here writing this in January 2016 and people are getting clobbered again by the decline of the stock market and the up-and-down roller coaster they ride every single day by investing in it. It's almost like rinse and repeat. It happened in 2000, 2001, 2002, 2008 and part of 2009.

Everybody got so used to the good old days of the last six years people forgot that stock markets actually really do move down sometimes and in a very dramatic fashion with their life savings struggling behind it. I don't see very many differences from the triggers that led up to the disaster of 2008, where a lot of people lost anywhere from 30% to 50% of their life savings. What I do see today is a lot of this same 'happy-go-lucky' attitude that was prevalent in 2008. As a result, many people got hammered because they were too overconfident about the stock market, housing market and the economy. You can see signs today of some of the very triggers in 2006 and 2007 that led to the 2008 market collapse.

What is different from 2008 is that the interest rate slot machine lever has been pulled all the way down by the Fed over the past several years. So now what is the recovery plan if we get into another 2008 style financial crisis? There isn't much interest rate lever left to pull, and in fact the Fed said it would probably go into a negative rate policy, something that has never been done in the history of our country.

Here are some of the signs that look eerily similar to the pre 2008 environment: housing markets exploding in value all over the U.S., multiple offers on homes in many areas at full asking price or above full asking price, a stock market that has hit all-time highs with encouragement from the 'experts' that it will continue its upside ride, banks trying to get you to take on more debt via credit cards and refinancing, low down or no down home purchase loans, no income verification loans and home builders building at a record pace.

What I've been telling people in my public speaking and workshops for the last two years is that the next great crash is going to be triggered by either China, Europe or another credit crisis and maybe even a combination of the two. Since August of 2015, you've seen China unprecedentedly devalue its currency, the Yuan, resulting in havoc and huge volatility on world stock exchanges.

Why is devaluation of China's currency bad for the U.S. and other countries? Because it makes our products and Europe's products more expensive to the rest of the world in comparison with China, where it is much less to buy product since they are devaluing their currency. What does this do to the prices and demand for goods and services from the U.S. and Europe? It makes them more expensive to other countries and China's products and services less expensive. This means potential manufacturing and growth slowdowns in the US and Europe.

Could the credit problems in the Eurozone potentially lead to the economic collapse of some of those countries and regions? What about the world's derivatives market, which has been estimated to be upwards of $700 trillion! Some analysts even put it at $1 Quadrillion! That is almost 10 to 15 times more than all the world's economies put together! However, approximately 95% of those derivatives remain unregulated, with nothing really to back them. These are the same type of derivatives that contributed to the downfall of Lehman Brothers and Bear Stearns in late 2008. In fact, the biggest culprit of these derivatives is the banking industry, where JP Morgan Chase owns over $70 trillion of them! However, they are 'off balance sheet', so when the Fed just completed their last stress test early last year of U.S. banks, they were shown to be financially sound.

The FDIC had a different take on that, however. They found that because these derivatives are 'off balance sheet', they are not included in the Fed's bank stress tests. If they were counted, none of the big U.S. banks would have passed the stress test. To give you an idea of how big JP Morgan Chase's derivative portfolio is, it is almost 3 times larger than the entire U.S. national debt, which currently is around $20 trillion. So how would Chase be able to make account holders whole or have enough reserves to cover losses if the derivatives market imploded? It's a scary but real thought.

Chapter 1

How Prepared Are You?

How prepared are you for retirement? The best way to know is to take the following retirement preparedness quiz. Be honest with yourself. It's ok if you cannot answer 'yes' to many of these questions.

In all of my years of practice, I still find it fascinating that many people do not understand their own money and how it works. Many people do not understand the amount of money they will need in retirement. Anyone who has ever believed any of the stuff they hear on television, or read in magazines and books about only needing 75% to 80% of their income in retirement is definitely living in a fantasy world.

What I have found is that many people need as much if not more than the income that they were making before they retired. The reason is because now they actually have the time to do the things that they always wanted to do but never had the time. They also now have the time to see their grandchildren and the people that they love and care about. All of this takes money. Travel is not cheap. Spending time with the grandkids may not be inexpensive either. Also, I find that people tend to eat out more, go to movies and plays more and do things that cost money to keep themselves entertained.

When you are working an 8 to 10 hour shift at work for 5 days a week, you do not have the luxury of doing a lot of these things like you do in retirement. Every one of my retired clients always mentions how busy they are in retirement and how they are busier now than when they were working a full-time job. But again, all of these things and activities cost money. Take the quiz on the next page and answer it honestly. Then let's discuss how you scored.

Retirement Preparedness Quiz

1. Do you know how much retirement income you will need to replace your current income and maintain your standard of living throughout retirement over the next 10, 20 or 30 years?

   YES   NO

2. Do you have a detailed written budget in place for the next 36 years which includes inflation and taxation impacts on your retirement income?

   YES   NO

3. Do you have any strategies within your retirement income plan that will continue to pay you a lifetime stream of income even if the balance of the account went to zero dollars?

   YES   NO

4. Do you know how rising long-term care costs could affect or destroy your retirement income plan?

   YES   NO

5. Do you have a 'tax transition' plan for your IRA to reduce or eliminate taxes on distributions?

   YES   NO

6. If you have a pension, do you know what happens to survivor income to your spouse and what percentage of income will be lost at your death?

   YES   NO

7. Do you know, based on the way your beneficiaries are currently titled within your 401(k) or IRA, if your children and grandchildren will inadvertently be disinherited?

   YES   NO

8. Do you know exactly how much in fees or commissions you're paying your advisor or broker each year?

   YES   NO

9. Do you know what percentage of your life savings would be lost in the market should another 2008 stock market decline happen again?

   YES   NO

Ok, now that you have taken the retirement preparedness quiz you have an idea of what it takes to get through and survive retirement. Remember, you could be spending more years in retirement than when you were working. By the time you retire, you will have most likely spent nearly 40 years working. If you retire at age 60, you could spend another 40 years in retirement if you live until age 100. How will you get through the next 40 years if you are operating purely on variables?

You're probably asking what I mean by 'variables'. The stock markct is a variable. There is no guarantee that the stock market is going to continue to go up in value every single year. Eventually, the market will correct… sometimes violently! If you are on the wrong side of the correction, you could stand to lose anywhere between 30% and 50% of your entire life savings!

When you were working and earning a paycheck from an employer you could afford the ups and downs of the market. You did not need the money yet, you were still working...you had income coming in. When you retire, you do not have the same luxury of a paycheck coming in. You're lucky if you get anything beyond Social Security income. Most people today do not have an old fashioned pension. Even if they do, there's no guarantee that will be enough income to live comfortably. The rest of your income needs to come from the money that you saved from working all those years and stashing away in your 401(k) and IRA.

The problem is that 401(k) and IRA money is all 'pretax' money. You never paid the IRS any taxes on the money that you put inside of your 401(k) or IRA. So you put the money into your 401(k) or IRA and you received a tax deduction or did not need to report income on the amount that you put into these types of accounts. The money grew tax-deferred and then you retired and started taking money out of these accounts. Every dollar you take out of these accounts is taxed as ordinary income, just like job income! I call it the seed and harvest theory. You received a tax break putting the seed money into these programs. The IRS reaps a huge benefit from you when you collect on what grew and turned into a harvest. Ultimately, Uncle Sam wins!

So let's break down some of the questions on the retirement preparedness quiz that you just took. Not outliving your money and also not becoming a partner to the IRS is very important.

How much retirement income will you need to replace your income that you made when you were working and maintain your standard of living over the next 10, 20, 30, or more years? Do you know? Have you ever done an analysis? Or did the firm or person that you're working with just sell you a bunch of financial products and you were not really sure how those coordinated and how much income those financial products would ultimately deliver you?

What about a budget? Do you have a written budget in place for the next 36 to 40 years which includes inflation and taxation impacts on your retirement income? Let's just use an inflation rate of 3% per year, which is what the government says is an average inflation rate over the last 30 to 40 years. In that case, that means that every 24 years you will need to double the amount of income that you are now receiving in order to keep the same lifestyle due to inflation. Sometimes people debate me on this fact but I bring up that they will need more income because costs shift as we get older.

For example, at age 60 or 65 you're probably still in pretty good health. But now let's take you to age 84 or 85. There may be a need for more medical treatment that Medicare may not cover. Also, some people would say that we are in a high tax bracket today as a country. What I need to remind them is that the United States, at certain times in its history, was at a top federal tax rate of 94% for the highest income earners. In fact, this was as recent as World War

II. Today, in 2016, the top federal tax rate is 39.6% for the highest income earners. This is quite a far cry from 94%. But it could get back to that someday due to all of the unfunded obligations that the government owes to its retirees. For example, all the people over the next 20 years that will be going onto Social Security and Medicare will definitely weigh down a system that is already near broke. The easiest lever that the government has at its disposal is to raise taxes to cover some of these obligations. If you have not factored in the tax picture on your 401(k) or IRA, you eventually might need a lot more income just to net the same amount due to increased taxation potentially.

Do you have any strategies within your retirement plan that will pay you a lifetime stream of income even if the asset goes to zero balance? This is important because many people are more ok with running out of money as long as they don't run out of income. Today, with the proper annuities, you can get guaranteed lifetime income even if the asset runs to zero balance. I know that the 'A' word is a bad word for many people in the media as they decide they want to pitch their stock market wares to retirees instead of encouraging them to find more guaranteed income. Annuities are not for everyone, but they can be a great source of lifetime income for those who have not saved enough for retirement or who might outlive their money due to life expectancy. Later on in this book I'll talk about the right kind of annuities and the wrong kind of annuities.

If you are lucky enough to have a pension from an employer, do you know what happens to survivor income to your spouse and whether or not they will get any income at all once you die, or will they be forced to take a haircut on the current income? This is very important and I deal with this issue with our retired clients on a daily basis. People always tell me they will not need as much income once one of the spouses passes. But I remind them that they will lose one of the Social Security benefits, in addition to losing or having a reduction of the pension income. In addition to that, I also remind them that since there is only one person now instead of two, there is an income shift a lot of times. Generally, it's easier to cook for two people than it is for one person and a lot of times it's easier for a single person to just eat out. Eating out costs money. In addition to that, many windows or widowers will want to keep socially involved and go out with their friends or family or take cruises or vacations with like-minded friends. This also costs money. I have a client that likes to constantly cruise. She lost her husband several years ago and since then she now goes on as many cruises as she can each year. The cruises that she goes on are typically 'six star' Radisson cruises. These cruises cost thousands of dollars per cruise and are inclusive of all alcohol, tips and excursions. She joyfully tells me, 'I'm spending my kids' inheritance'. So making up the income deficiency that is lost when one of the spouses passes is critical. You have to have strategies in place in order to make up this income deficiency.

Do you know, based on the way your beneficiaries are currently titled within your 401(k) or IRA, if your kids or grandkids will inadvertently be disinherited? When is the last time that you or your advisor reviewed your beneficiary form for your IRA? Or, when was the last time you checked your 401(k) beneficiary form on your 401(k) plan at work?

A while back, a couple came into our office as a referral from an existing client. After reviewing their statements from their broker, I had them back in the office and was concerned that there did not appear to be a contingent beneficiary on their IRA accounts. You see, many spouses are primary beneficiary of each other. If something happens to both of them jointly, they need to have a contingent beneficiary on the IRA or 401(k) account. In this case, there did not appear to be a contingent beneficiary. We proceeded to call the broker on the telephone via a three-way call. The wife asked the broker if there was a contingent beneficiary and then I heard a long pregnant pause on the telephone. About 30 seconds later, the broker came back on the phone and said there was no contingent beneficiary on hers or her husband's IRA accounts. His reasoning for this lack of contingent beneficiaries was because in 30 years of his being a stockbroker, he has never seen two spouses who have died together in an accident. What!? Actually, this couple had just finished telling me a story about how they were on a bus together in Spain when there was an accident that sent several people to the hospital. What if that crash had led to a fatality?

It's so easy to name a contingent beneficiary. It is simply a name, date of birth, Social Security number and percentage of benefit. As a result of this stockbroker's negligence, their kids and grandchildren would have been disinherited should something have happened to both of them. Their case would've ended up in probate court and their kids would've had to wait 1 to 2 years for a judge to determine who would've benefitted from their IRA accounts. You need to make sure your beneficiaries are titled the right way.

How much in fees and commissions are you paying your advisor or broker every year? Most people cannot answer this. What I do is a detailed cost analysis of what they are paying in fees or commissions to their financial person. Sometimes people are shocked how much they are actually paying. Many times they are paying an advisory fee on top of a mutual fund fee if they own a lot of mutual funds within their account.

Finally, what percentage of your life savings would be lost in another repeat of the tech bubble bursting in the year 2000 or a repeat of the 2008 credit crisis? Both times, I saw some people walk into my office who lost 50% of their life savings! How do you make up that loss if you are in retirement? You need to make sure that you understand how far down your account can go in the next market crash. Then you need to take steps to correct that problem. What I provide for people who meet with me is an analysis of their accounts to find out what their maximum loss would be in the case of a major market decline. I then provide them solutions to correct the problem. This is important information to know.

Chapter 2

The Importance of a Budget:

Now that you've taken the Retirement Preparedness Quiz in the previous chapter and understand how important a lot of those questions are when considering whether or not you can retire, it is now time for us to talk about the importance of a budget in an overall retirement income plan.

How can any financial advisor or stockbroker sell you products when they don't even know how much you'll need to spend? I see this happen way too many times in my industry…products are sold to clients and they don't even understand how the product fits into an overall retirement income plan. Most firms and people in my business don't have a clue how to design retirement income plans. All they are good at is selling you product. You first have to understand how much you will need in retirement and then center the plan around that.

I can't stress the importance of having a budget when you get into retirement. I've had some people tell me, 'Mark I don't want to be restricted to a budget', and my answer to that is 'You're not limiting yourself to a budget, you're building a framework for yourself so that you do not overspend and run out of money in retirement!'

I have had people who come into me who continue to spend like they are still working even though they are now retired. You cannot continue to spend like you did before you retired, without having certain limits set. I even had one gentleman come in and tell me that he and his wife could not live off of less than $350,000 per year, even though he only saved up about $3,500,000 for retirement. Upon my calculations they would be out of money in about 12 to 15 years.

When they were working they could easily spend that because both were pulling in a combined total income of around $400,000 per year from their employers. That kind of income put them in the top 5% of income earners in the United States and therefore they could spend like that. But now they need to be a little bit more realistic.

This couple has been a client of mine for nearly four years and we have had three budget revisions since they first came on board with my firm. This most recent and final budget revision was after he finally retired. His wife retired about a year ago. After going through the numbers with the husband and helping him understand that they would run out of money in 12 to 15 years, I told him they had to cut approximately $75,000 each year out of that $350,000 budget that they would like to have. By doing this and also by taking his pension the correct way, they were now able to extend that 12 year retirement life cycle to over 35 years without running short of income.

By helping him understand all the variables, building in various lifetime income strategies into their plan and getting a better grasp on their budget, he now feels much more at ease and that retirement for him and his wife is really achievable.

I've put together a proprietary budget tool that you can use and that we step our clients through when creating a budget. It analyzes inflation and tax impacts on your income needs over the next 36 years. It includes all the categories that you need for both required expenses and for what I call lifestyle expenses.

Required expenses are expenses for things we need in order to have a basic lifestyle. They include things like mortgage payments, property taxes, insurances, utilities, groceries, clothing, auto expenses, etc.

Lifestyle expenses are expenses which include travel and things that are not required for you to survive. You can even put in rental expenses from rental properties and rental income. You can also model the expense year-by-year. Say for example that your kids' college expenses are going to be over four years…you can put that in an 'other' category, rename the category and flow the expenses for four years.

On the analysis tab it will show you how much income gap you will have after accounting for all of your expenses and income. The income gap is the amount of money you will need to pull from your retirement savings on a year-by-year basis.

The program will show you your true retirement income gap. Go to my website at **www.retirementbudgettool.com** and you can download this great program for free!

Chapter 3

How Long Will I Need My Money To Last?

The new 4% rule is really 2%. In the last chapter I talked about the importance of having a budget in retirement. The old rule that you could spend 4% per year of your savings when you retire and still be fine in retirement has been replaced with a new 2% rule.

This recent study was conducted by Dr. Wade Pfau, a professor of retirement income at the American College and financial advisor Wade Dokken.* The study shows that you would likely run out of money before life expectancy by spending 4% per year from your savings because of the uncontrollable impacts of large up-and-down stock market swings and a lagging low interest-rate environment.

But it really is worse than that. Planning for life expectancy is just not enough. People today are living to age 100 in increasing numbers. There are more 'centenarians' than ever before. In fact, one of the largest segments of the population for growth relative to its size is the over age 80 population.

So if you only plan for a lifespan of 80 to 85 years old, you could be cutting yourself short by 15 to 20 years! All the studies that are done are based on lifespan and life expectancy. But what they do not take into account is someone living to age 100.

So think about it, for the last 35 to 40 years you worked for employer and had a steady paycheck coming in. Now for the next 35 to 40 years of retirement you are going to be the paycheck.

This is why you cannot overspend in the beginning of retirement. Overspending will literally kill your retirement savings later on when you need it the most.

*Wade Pfau and Wade Dokken, "Why 4% Could Fail." Financial Advisor Magazine, Sept. 2015

Chapter 4

The Pitfalls of Unknown Variables in Retirement:

The up and down roller coaster stock market is not a solid predictable vehicle to get you through retirement and it has many variables that could cause you to lose your life savings if your timing is not just right. Huge stock market swings, publicly traded companies going out of business, stock prices crashing, companies cutting dividends…that's the risk you take when you put all your eggs in the stock market basket!

I always hear the same things from people in or nearing retirement who visit me for help..."Why can't I make money in this market?"..."Why can't I have a steady stream of income coming in?"..."It seems like the market is a constant roller coaster".

You see since the early 1980s the government has put you in charge of your retirement plan at work. That plan is called a 401(k). These workplace retirement plans have, in most cases, very limited mutual funds and nobody really watching the farm. The government also expects you to be an expert at managing your own money! Who would expect you to be an expert at anything else in life that you have no training for?

Think about it, would you do dental work on yourself? What about doing your own heart surgery? So how can the government then expect you, somebody who really knows nothing about managing money on Wall Street or who has never had formal training of such, to manage their own retirement life savings? Unless you've had specialized training in sophisticated stock market strategies or have worked on the floor of the stock exchange, any money you have made in the stock market over the years really is 'pure luck'…or being at 'the right place at the right time'.

To prove my point, how far down did your investment portfolio go in 2008 and in the early part of 2009 before it recovered? I bet for most of you, that number is anywhere between a low of 25% to a high of a 60% decline in the value of your portfolio. Then you try to justify it and say, "But the stock market came back". To that, I say, that's great self-justification. But the stock market may not come back as quickly the next time around. What was the main reason the market came back so quickly after the enormous declines in 2008 and early 2009? The reason is because the Fed lowered the interest rate environment nearly twenty times to accommodate an interest rate policy of essentially 'free money'. That nearly free money drove corporations and hedge funds to borrow at very low interest rates and then take the money they borrowed and use their talent to make thousands of percent gain on that very same money that they borrowed from the Fed at a very low cost.

However, this interest rate environment is a huge danger if we have anything close to another 2008 meltdown. What lever can the fed pull next time if we do get into a repeat of 2008? Interest rates have been battered so low from the Fed's quantitative easing policy over the last several years, there would not be a lot of room for the Fed to move rates much lower to counterbalance another Great Recession. We then could be looking at a prolonged flat sideways type of stock market and maybe not see recovery for many many years out.

I'll prove my point using the next chart. The next chart shows how many years your money would've been in a sideways pattern in previous flat markets and what the total rate of return on your money would have been over that period of years. For example, you can see from 1929 to 1954 you would've essentially made no money in the stock market. The same could be said from 1966 to 1982. Also, if you look at our stock market's most recent sideways pattern from 2000 to 2012, you would've hardly made any return in the U.S. stock market. With that kind of reality, how can anyone justify using the stock market as a reliable investment strategy to get you through the next 30 or 40 years of retirement?

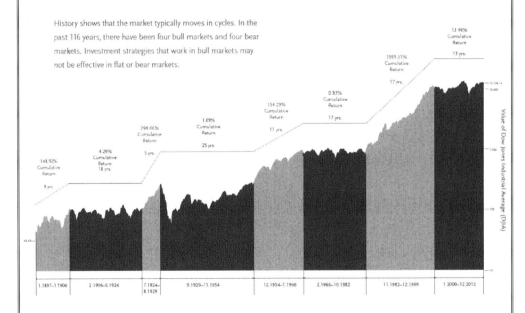

History shows that the market typically moves in cycles. In the past 116 years, there have been four bull markets and four bear markets. Investment strategies that work in bull markets may not be effective in flat or bear markets.

148.92% Cumulative Return
9 yrs.

4.29% Cumulative Return
18 yrs.

294.66% Cumulative Return
5 yrs.

1.69% Cumulative Return
25 yrs.

154.29% Cumulative Return
11 yrs.

0.83% Cumulative Return
17 yrs.

1059.31% Cumulative Return
17 yrs.

13.98% Cumulative Return
13 yrs.

Value of Dow Jones Industrial Average (DJIA)

1. 1897–1.1906 | 2. 1906–6.1924 | 7.1924–8.1929 | 9.1929–11.1954 | 12.1954–1.1966 | 2.1966–10.1982 | 11.1982–12.1999 | 1.2000–12.2012

SOURCE: Graph created by Guggenheim Investments using data from dowjones.com. Logarithmic graph of the Dow Jones Industrial Average from 1.1897 through 12.2012. Performance displayed represents past performance, which is no guarantee of future results. For more information call 800.820.0888 or visit guggenheiminvestments.com.

Chapter 5

The Negative Effects of Reverse Dollar Cost Averaging:

Dollar cost averaging can be defined as investing money in the market at various times instead of all at once and therefore have a smoother overall entry point. Dollar cost averaging can allow you to incrementally invest money at different periods, allowing you to get more purchasing power when the stock market tanks and less purchasing power when the stock market is high. It is said to be a better alternative to trying to time the market. Over a long period of time this approach has proven to work well for many investors.

But there is a reverse to this method called 'reverse dollar cost averaging' which happens once you're in retirement and using the money that you've saved and dollar cost averaged into the market all of your working years. When you are retired, you need money to live off of. So it is no longer an 'accumulation' savings approach to retirement for you. Instead, it becomes a 'distribution' spending approach in retirement. You'll be using the money you saved to live off of. Reverse dollar cost averaging can be devastating to a retirement. The reason is this…You cannot effectively time the stock market and sell at the most opportune time. You may need money next month and need to sell into a market low.

That's how 'reverse dollar cost averaging' works. You start to 'dollar cost distribute' out of the market the money that you have saved. So in a low and depressed market you may be forced to sell more shares of a depressed mutual fund or stock to net the same amount of cash, versus selling that same stock or mutual fund in an 'up' market or when the market is high. This is called 'reverse dollar cost averaging'. Also, there is something else that happens to your retirement savings when reverse dollar cost averaging occurs. Because you had to sell more shares of your stock or mutual funds, you have less shares to go back up in value when the stock market finally does recover. Therefore, you may never recover!

For instance, let's look at the impact a 20% loss in your portfolio could have if you need money to live off of and the effects of 'reverse dollar cost averaging' are felt:

Value of account before 20% portfolio
stock market loss: $100,000

Value of account after 20% portfolio
stock market loss: $80,000

Cash needed from portfolio: $5,000

New value of balance after withdrawal: $75,000

Percentage needed to recover your
portfolio back to the original $100,000: 34%

This means you need a 9% greater return on top of recovering the 20% loss and the $5,000 withdrawal from the original balance before the stock market crashed just to get back to break even. Hopefully, you get my point.

Being in the stock market in a moderate or even more aggressive portfolio is fine, but you better have that piece of the portfolio for the right income stage of retirement. I like to put it at the back end of retirement instead of the front end. This way, if you are needing money from investments to live off of, you can afford to take a large stock market decline on that account, since I build the moderate portfolio to be a portfolio that you will not need to access for many many years. Therefore, even if the market goes down, you have many years to recover that loss and bring the account back up.

I learned this lesson in 2008 when I witnessed a lot of people sell out of the market at the worst possible time. They sold out at all-time lows. They then missed the corresponding run-up in the market over the next 6 years, in a market which has been the second longest bull market in history thus far. Had their money been positioned correctly in the right stages and risk tolerance so they didn't need to sell out of accounts that lost a lot of value in order to get their income, they would've likely recovered above where they were when their accounts had previously hit an all-time high.

How can you avoid or reduce the effects of reverse dollar cost averaging from happening to your portfolio? Later in this book I'm going to share with you a strategy called the 'Retirement Income Wheel' which will show you how to properly stage your income in retirement.

Chapter 6

Institutional Versus Retail:

There is a definite difference between institutional wealth management and retail wealth management. I classify retail wealth management mainly as mutual funds. When a fund manager becomes good enough, generally they'll break off and start their own institutional management team. Institutional wealth management gives you the ability to play with the big boys, whereas retail mutual funds are mainly designed for people who are just entering the investing world.

Retail mutual funds can be quite expensive and all the costs are not disclosed inside of what they call a prospectus. Whereas, with institutional wealth management, all the costs are disclosed and fully transparent. So how do retail mutual funds differ from institutional wealth management?

First, with retail mutual funds you only own a share of the fund. With institutional wealth management in separate managed accounts (SMAs), you actually own the stock or the asset inside of the portfolio and it is registered to you in your name. The advantage of this is that you can 'tax loss harvest' inside of an institutional account where it is fairly difficult to do this inside of the retail mutual fund. For example, let's say that I have certain positions that are up in value for the year inside of my institutional account and I have other positions that are down in value for the year in that same account. At the end of the year I can look at my institutional account and figure which positions have gains and which positions have losses. I can then use the positions in the account that have losses to offset the ones that have gains, thereby creating a 'wash' environment, or break even, for taxes.

Also, you can avoid paying capital gains tax now on a particular stock and choose to pay it when you want within an institutional account. Let's say that a retail mutual fund owned XYZ stock. Over the years that you've owned this institutional account, XYZ stock has done very well. You then decide to get out of the institutional managed account and do something else with the money. In any retail mutual fund, XYZ stock would need to be sold in order to get you your cash. However, in an institutional portfolio, you can segregate XYZ stock and put it in its own 'non-billed' self-managed account and keep the stock as long as you want without triggering any kind of capital gain until you're ready to sell.

Additionally, with institutional accounts, you're basically paying a flat fee for the amount of assets managed. It doesn't matter what type of portfolio you are in with the manager, you're paying the same fee. Therefore, there is no incentive to the advisor to put you in one portfolio over the other to pad their pocket. The advisor is on a level playing field. He or she does not benefit from putting you in one portfolio over another portfolio. Therefore, commission conflicts of interest are eliminated.

However, with retail mutual funds there is an incentive for the advisor to put you in certain funds over other funds. Mutual funds come in four 'share' class categories. The first share class is institutional. With an institutional class of mutual fund, that is what a large institution would invest in and get significant discounts by investing in that particular share class of the fund due to the large amount of money the institution would invest.

The second share class is an 'A' share class. Typically, this share class of funds is known as 'front loaded'. The load, is a commission which goes to the brokerage firm and is typically anywhere between 4% and 5% of the purchase price when you invest in the fund. For example, let's say that you invest $100,000 into an A share fund.

You will pay the brokerage firm a $4,000 or $5,000 upfront commission to get into the fund. You then do not start with $100,000, you start with less, maybe $96,000 or $95,000. So out of the gate, you are already down on your money and trying to play catch-up. Combine that with a potential market loss and you could be in real trouble.

The third share class of funds is a 'B' share class. With a B share class of funds you typically do not have an upfront commission but you have a back end commission called a contingent deferred sales charge or CDSC. The problem with this B class share is that the broker will tell you that you don't have a front loaded commission, which is true. But this share class of fund is loaded from the backend. The way the brokerage firm makes money is from a higher 12b1 fee. A 12b1 fee is an 'advertising charge'. This 'advertising charge' is typically 75% higher in a B share class of mutual funds. So the broker is sucking more out of your balance every year to pay the advertising charge. Isn't it nice that you get to pay the advertising charge for mutual funds? So instead of the broker getting 4% or 5% upfront, they just continue to get this increased advertising charge on the back end for a number of years. Typically, after six or seven years most of these B share funds will convert to an A share class of fund. Now, after they convert to an A share, if you invest more money you'll be hit again with the 4% to 5% upfront commission charge that the A share class charges. It is typically in the brokerage firm's best interest to sell you a B share fund. They make more over time than they would if they just sold you an upfront loaded A share fund.

The fourth class of funds is called a 'C' share class of mutual funds. This class of mutual funds is typically referred to as 'level loaded'. There could be a small front end load, much lower than an A share fund but still a small load nonetheless. These funds also carry the 75% greater 12b1 advertising charge. However the 12b1 fee never goes away in a C share class of funds. This share class never converts to an A share class. So the brokerage firm is always making money every year as long as you own the fund.

It's sort of like when you were in school. If the teacher gave you an A+ grade, that meant that you were a really good student. That would be like an institutional share class mutual fund. If the teacher gave you an A or A-, that meant that you were still a good student. That would be like an A share class mutual fund. If you were an ok student, the teacher would typically give you a B grade. That would be like a B share class mutual fund. Finally, if you were not that good of a student then the teacher would give you a C grade. You still passed the class, but you would not have the grades to get you into Harvard or Yale. Think of this C grade as the C share class of mutual funds.

Many brokerage firms have been sued over the years by their investors for putting them in the B share and C share mutual fund classes. These firms have also been heavily fined by industry regulators for putting people in these classes of funds that put more money into the brokerage firms' pockets and less into the consumers.

Then there are also markups and markdowns in mutual funds and soft dollar payments. A markup would be defined as taking in a particular stock for a certain price and then charging a higher price to the owners of the fund to buy that stock. Who keeps the spread? You guessed it, the mutual fund. A markdown, would be the opposite. When a mutual fund sells a particular stock they can sell it at a price that is higher than what they are giving the owners of the fund. Again, they keep the spread.

A 'soft dollar' incentive can occur if a mutual fund offers to pay for research from a brokerage firm by executing trades at that brokerage. For an example, if ABC Small Cap Mutual Fund wants to buy some research from XYZ Brokerage Firm, ABC fund may agree to spend $5,000 in commissions for brokerage services in return for research from XYZ Brokerage Firm. This would be considered a soft dollar payment.

Certain brokerage firms also have exclusive arrangements with certain mutual fund companies and get higher commissions as a result. One of the well-known brokerage firms that does this is Edward Jones. Every time I see an Edward Jones client come to me for help I always tell them "I bet you own American Funds".

The other way mutual funds can get you is turnover costs. Turnover costs are defined as the churning or buying and selling inside of a fund of its positions. A manager might do this to try to keep the fund's rate of return competitive or may also do this because they can then take markups and markdowns on those bought and sold positions. Nonetheless, it is expensive for the consumer. Some mutual funds I've seen have had turnover of 300% or 400% in a given year. What this means to the consumer is that particular fund is selling and buying everything 3 to 4 times within a given 12 month period! Who pays all those costs? You do!

None of these 12b1 fees, soft dollar incentives, turnover costs, markups and markdowns, or other incentives can be written off by you, the consumer, even though you're paying them in mutual fund costs. The IRS doesn't allow you to deduct these as management fees. Also, the SEC does not require disclosure of many of these costs either. So you really don't know what you're paying. The prospectus doesn't tell the full story. The SEC doesn't require it to.

Now, contrast everything that you've learned about mutual funds with institutional wealth management. In institutional wealth management, you would typically go through a Registered Investment Advisor firm to get access to institutional wealth managers who also typically operate as Registered Investment Advisors. Unlike retail mutual funds, there is a fiduciary relationship that is created when you work with a Registered Investment Advisor. For these institutional wealth managers, it is about the getting the best price and execution of a particular stock or holding. Soft dollar costs and markups and markdowns are not allowed. The SEC prohibits these practices. So, in a portfolio when the institutional manager is buying or selling, they are doing it at the lowest possible trading cost and attempting to get you the best deal. Also, since you are paying a flat fee for management, there is no incentive to sell you a higher commission portfolio. Commissions don't exist on the institutional side, therefore there is no monetary incentive for the advisor to direct you to one portfolio over another. It's an even playing field.

The fiduciary relationship that is created dictates the advisor do what is in the client's best interest and not their own. This is a far cry from the commission based salespeople hired by banks and brokerage firms who do not have to operate from a fiduciary standpoint, but simply from a 'suitability' standpoint. The entity who usually determines 'suitability' is the broker or the brokerage firm. If it can pad their pocket, then the sale is probably deemed 'suitable' although it may not be fiduciarily responsible and in the best interest of the client.

Additionally, in most cases, institutional management fees can be written off on a tax return…unlike mutual funds, where they cannot be. This can bring the overall cost of doing business down for the average consumer comparative to mutual funds.

Chapter 7

The Low Interest Rate Dilemma:

How do you live today as a retiree on these terrible low interest rates that have occurred over the last few years? I remember a time when you could go to the bank and get 5% to 6% interest on your money. Weren't those the good old days? Nowadays, you go to the bank and you're lucky to get a .5% to 1% interest rate on your money! Just to eek out $20,000 per year of income…if you had all your money at the bank, you would need to have $2 million parked at the bank if you are earning only 1%!

The reality is our country is better than most today. In fact if you go to Europe, some of those countries have a negative interest-rate environment. Meaning that if you put your money away in a bank you would actually get negative interest! In fact in Japan, their 10 year treasury rate just fell to .1% as I am writing this book. That's one tenth of 1%! That means for 10 years, you would get one tenth of 1% if you locked your money up in a Japanese 10 year treasury bond!

So where does one go today to get any kind of interest or yield on their money? The best place and most liquid place to get yield today is certain high dividend paying stocks. For an example, a stock like AT&T gets upwards of 5% yield per year! What this means, is that even if the price of AT&T stock does nothing, the owner of that stock will still get 5% that year. Think about it like a rent check coming in from your stock. This yield on stocks is referred to as a 'dividend'. A dividend is a payment to the owner of a particular company's stock from profits that the company makes.

Owning a dividend paying stock can also be helpful in a stock market decline. If the price of the stock goes down 5% but the dividend is 5%, then essentially the consumer has lost really nothing that year. The dividend can help counterbalance a loss in the stock. Not all stocks are dividend paying. You have to identify what you want your portfolio to do before you buy any stock or go into any type of investment.

High-yield bonds can also be a source of good income, however you need to be careful because they are much more volatile than a typical bond. The price of the high-yield bond can go down a lot more rapidly and therefore you could take a loss on your bond portfolio if you need the money before the bond matures. But with the right management team and the right portfolio, a good mix of high dividend paying stocks and high-yield bonds can be a good way to overcome the low interest rate dilemma.

With my clients, I like to use dividend and yield based accounts like this on the front end of a retirement. They typically have less volatility and are less risky than accounts with stocks that do not pay dividends nor have a concentration of bonds. When I design an income plan, typically I will use this type of dividend and yielding account as a 'stage one' income account for a client in retirement. I will explain more of that later in the book.

The reason why a lot of people get hurt during retirement is they don't change their strategy from a moderate strategy to a more conservative strategy when they start taking income. A market decline can take their portfolio way down if they are in moderate accounts and then the combination of also pulling money from those accounts to live off of can further devastate the portfolio.

The proper time to use a moderate account in retirement is at the back end of retirement. I use this as a 'stage three' income strategy within an overall retirement income plan. The reason why people get so beat up in the market and lose huge amounts of money in big stock market declines is because they are needing to withdraw out of a moderate account too early. If they transition the moderate account to the last stage of retirement then they have the time to let the market make up the loss and generate returns.

I like to train my clients to not worry about their moderate accounts when the market goes down because they are not going to typically need this money for years and years out…the way that I design the income plan. So, what is happening this month or next month or even this year in the market is really no consequence to them in the longer-term. If they are in retirement for 20 or 30 years and we don't need the moderate account income for 10 to 15 years, then there really is no worry if the stock market has a huge drop right now.

So if a conservative account is a stage one income account in retirement, and a moderate account is a stage three income account in retirement, then what is the centerpiece of retirement income, or 'stage two'? For stage two, typically I like to use the proper type of annuities with certain guaranteed income riders. Now I know what you are saying, "Mark I have heard so many bad things about annuities and that I should stay away from them". With certain types of annuities, I would most certainly agree with that statement.

However not all annuities are bad. I liken annuities to fruit. When you go to the store there is a lot of different kind of fruit that you can buy. It does not mean that you need to like every type of fruit. I might like oranges, but I might not like cherries. However, both are fruit. I hate it when the media, or people that don't really understand the income planning world, put down annuities and make all annuities seem as though they are bad.

For those people who are the annuity haters, I have to ask the question, "Do you not like your Social Security check?" Because Social Security really is an annuity payment from the federal government to you on a monthly basis as long as you live! Or, let's take a person who has a pension coming in from their employer for the rest of their life. That pension check really is an annuity payment. Or, let's use the lottery as an example. If you were lucky enough to win the lottery you could choose to have your winnings paid over a period of years. Those annual payments are essentially an annuity.

So not all annuities are bad. It's just the way that annuities are used by the financial industry that makes them bad sometimes. When you have your bank's financial salesperson trying to sell you an annuity with no income plan around it, it's bad. When you have your stockbroker at a major brokerage firm, who is trying to sell you a variable annuity because they make a high commission, you pay a ton of fees and there is no plan around it…then it is bad. But, what if we could use annuities to drive income into our retirement for the rest of our life. Then wouldn't annuities be good?

You see, annuities should never be used as an accumulation type of product or strategy. Annuities are meant to be an eventual payout product or strategy. But you have to be careful, you cannot turn on the income too quickly in an annuity because annuities are driven by mortality. Mortality is how long you're expected to live. The older you become, the less mortality you have. So annuities are driven by mortality factors.

I can compare this example to Social Security. If you turn on Social Security income too soon your paycheck will be less. If you turn on Social Security income later, your check will be more. It's not that Social Security is able to make more on your money because you delay taking it. They can pay you more because you have less life expectancy to live. Again, this is called mortality.

Life insurance companies sell annuities. Over the last several hundred years that these life insurance companies have been in business, they've hired very smart people called actuaries to figure out when a general population will die based on age. These smart actuaries are responsible for determining the mortality income payout factors of annuities. In the next chapter, I'm going to talk about annuities more in depth and how they can complement an income plan. But, as I said before, the annuity needs to be the right kind of annuity.

Chapter 8

Annuities…The Good, The Bad, The Ugly:

As I mentioned in the last chapter, annuities can be a good complement to a retirement income plan. But they have to be the right kind of annuity.

Being in this business for 22 years now has taught me a lot. The first thing it has taught me is to read a contract. The second thing it has taught me is that most people in my industry do not read contracts. Therefore, when they sell an annuity, which is a contract between the insurance company and the individual buying it, most advisors or financial salespeople don't know what the heck they are putting a client into.

Here is how it all works...the insurance company tries to use all the gimmicks that they can to get financial advisors and financial salespeople to sell their products. The insurance companies tell these advisors or financial salespeople all the great things that will benefit the client in that particular annuity contract. What the insurance companies do not do is go through all the cons of that particular annuity contract with the people selling the product.

So in a desperation to make a sales quota or make their rent, the financial salesperson or financial advisor goes and sells all the 'hype' that they were told by the insurance company about all the great things that this particular annuity can do for the client. But the advisor or salesperson doesn't read the annuity contract. I cannot tell you how many times I have had people come into my office who have bought annuities from other people in my industry who have never read the contract…and they think they bought something that they don't really own.

This is what gives the annuity industry a bad name, advisors and agents who don't educate their client on what the client is really buying and the cons along with the pros. These same people who come into my office who do not understand what they own, because they were told wrong information by the person who sold them the annuity, are furious that they bought this particular type of annuity contract and feel like they've been ripped off or taken advantage of. This is how annuity companies and annuity agents and salespeople get into lawsuits. If they had just read the darn contract! There are so many variables that you need to consider when buying an annuity.

There are basically four types of annuities. The first kind is called an 'Immediate Annuity'. With this type of an annuity, you give up all of your money to the insurance company in exchange for a payment stream of income for the rest of your life or for a period of years. The problem with Immediate Annuities is that it's like getting your own money back. If you don't live long enough, then basically the insurance company could end up keeping the money depending on the distribution strategy that you choose. I typically never recommend this type of an annuity for clients.

The second type of an annuity is called a deferred annuity. There are two types of deferred annuities: fixed and variable. First, let's talk about the deferred Variable Annuity. There is a company that does a lot of advertising and who wants your money to manage. The person that runs that company is a guy by the name of Ken Fisher. He puts all these negative articles out about annuities and tries to incentivize you to not buy annuities. A simple reason for this is because he would like to make more in fees off your money every single year…over a period of years, instead of you channeling that money to the insurance company where he will never see a dime of fees. The reality, is that he does have some good points.

The annuities that he describes in all of his literature are Variable Annuities. The problem with that literature is that it makes it seem like every annuity is a Variable Annuity. If you are not in the financial services industry and you cannot discern what type of an annuity he is referring to, then you will think that all annuities are bad. Years ago when I had a stockbroker's license (before I became a fiduciary), I was told by the firm that I worked for that I had to sell these monstrous investments to my clients. I was even fired from one firm because I refused to sell Variable Annuities to clients. This is one of the reasons why I became a fiduciary and started my own Registered Investment Advisor firm, so that I did not ever have to sell another one of these again.

Before I became educated in the annuity world, I was told that these Variable Annuities would be great for clients because they could take advantage of the stock market and also have a death benefit wrapper around their investment. For example, if a client invested $100,000 into one of these annuities and the stock market lost 30% and then the client died the next day, instead of their beneficiary receiving $70,000 the beneficiary would get $100,000. On the surface this sounds great! The reality is that there is a huge charge for that benefit…it's called a mortality and expense charge, or commonly referred to as an M&E fee. Essentially, it's overpriced life insurance.

Then, in addition to that fee, you have a lot of other fees within that type of an annuity. Some of the other common fees in every Variable Annuity contract are administrative expenses, management fees for the mutual fund like subaccounts, and other rider charges. At the end of the day, an average Variable Annuity can have anywhere between 2% and 5% in charges each year by the time you add them all up.

Here is what that means to the average consumer. Let's assume that the Variable Annuity only made enough money each year just to cover the fees and expenses. Let's assume that the initial investment was $100,000. So that $100,000 would remain constant through the life of the annuity contract. I am assuming that the fees would be covered by gains, but nothing more beyond that. Remember, I said the average fees in a Variable Annuity can range from 2% up to 5% or more. So let's take a median between those two numbers as a fee. That fee would then represent 3.5% per year. On a $100,000 annuity, assuming that the only growth in that annuity was enough to cover fees, it would mean $3,500 per year of fees each and every year that you own the annuity contract. Over a ten-year period, that adds up to $35,000. Over a 20 year period, that adds up to $70,000!

So over a 20 year period of owning a Variable Annuity, you could be paying over 70% or more of your initial investment in fees! Because of this, I do agree with Ken Fisher that you should stay away from Variable Annuities. But, there is another cousin of this deferred Variable Annuity called a deferred Fixed Annuity or a deferred Fixed Index Annuity. These are the third and fourth types of annuities that I will discuss next.

What is a deferred Fixed Annuity or a deferred Fixed Index Annuity? Essentially, both of these are like bank accounts with an insurance company. Instead of you putting your money in ABC Bank, you're putting your money in ABC Insurance Company. When you buy these two types of annuities you never have any risk of stock market loss within your account. Also, there are no fees on these types of annuities, unless you buy an optional income rider which I will discuss later. These are the types of annuities that I use within an overall retirement income plan.

The difference between the Fixed Annuity and the Fixed Index Annuity is that the Fixed Annuity pays a stated rate of interest each year just like a bank would pay you. Some years the interest could be more, some years the interest could be less. The problem today is that interest rates in Fixed Annuities, while not as low as the bank, are still relatively low compared to long-term interest rates. So you do not want to get stuck into a low interest-rate annuity in today's low interest-rate environment.

The Fixed Index Annuity, however, has an interest rate that can tie to the performance of a stock market index. But unlike the Variable Annuity, you can never lose any of your principal balance due to stock market declines because you're not actually in the stock market. The downside with this product is that you do not get the full increase of the index in a particular year. For example, let's say that you decide you want to link your Fixed Index Annuity to the S&P 500 index. Let's assume that the S&P 500 for that year went up 10%. In a Fixed Index Annuity, you may get only 2.5% or 3%. This is called a 'cap' in the product. The insurance company will pay you everything up to 2.5% or 3% of the total gain of the S&P 500. However, the upside potential may be better than the fixed interest rate that a Fixed Annuity may pay you. Also, if you were to earn 2.5% or 3% in a given year, isn't that better than what the bank would pay you?

So the real comparison with this type of product should be a comparison with bank interest rates, not the stock market. Your money is always principal protected. The worst you can do in a down market year is to post a 0% rate of return on your annuity for that year in a Fixed Index Annuity. Versus the earlier Variable Annuity that we talked about, whereby you could lose much of your life savings in a major decline market year. I use Fixed Index Annuities for safety of principal while also allowing the client to get some level of interest posted to their account. However, because of the low interest-rate environment today and the low cap rates within a lot of these products today, I use this product as an income only strategy with clients in an overall income plan. They are not really designed to be great accumulation accounts, but they are designed to be great income payout accounts.

So then how do I use a Fixed Index Annuity today when designing an overall retirement income plan for a client? Some of these products today feature something called an 'income rider'. For a small charge each year the client has a separate calculation of value if they use the annuity eventually as an income stream and take the money out in payments.

How does this differ from an Immediate Annuity? In an Immediate Annuity, I lose all access to my principal balance and only get income payments for my lifetime or a period of years. If I have a financial emergency, I cannot go back to the insurance company and tell them I want my remaining principal balance back. Also, if I buy a Fixed Index Annuity or a regular Fixed Annuity and do not buy the optional income rider, if I do turn one of these on for lifetime income it then functions like the Immediate Annuity…whereby I would lose all access to my principal balance and can never get to it if I have a financial emergency.

Therefore, I will not typically put a client in a Fixed Index Annuity or Fixed Annuity today unless we combine that with the optional income rider. When the client turns on the optional income rider for income, then they will get a payment stream over their lifetime or they can also select the joint lifetime option for themselves and their spouse if they are married. If they ever get into a financial bind, they can stop the income payments and take the remaining principal balance out of the annuity. So they always have access to their cash. Also, when they die, the insurance company does not keep the remaining balance of the annuity. Their beneficiaries will get that in a lump sum, if they desire.

So now think about the Fixed Index Annuity or the Fixed Annuity with an income rider…it's like a bank account that will pay out a lifetime of income where the income will never run out even if the balance does! If you don't spend through all the balance, your beneficiary gets the remaining balance at your death. So again, it's like you are drawing from a bank account then eventually dying and leaving the balance of that bank account to your beneficiary. There is no penalty for the beneficiary to take the lump sum balance.

The other thing that is important to know about income riders is that before you decide to take the money as income, the optional income rider has an income value separate from the actual value of the annuity. This separate value is commonly referred to as an accounting value within the annuity contract. So when you get your statement each year it will show two values on the statement. The first value will be your actual or real value that you posted interest on that year. The second value will be a guaranteed income value, that if you use it eventually for income then it is growing at a certain percentage interest rate each and every year…compounding until you turn it on for income.

For example, some of the companies today offer anywhere between 5.5% to 7% as a compounding guaranteed rate of return each year on the income value. What this means to you, the owner of the annuity contract, is even if the interest rate environment remains terribly low or the stock market implodes over a period of years, your value will continue to go up at this 5.5% or 7% rate until you take it as income. This means that when you do turn on income payments, you have a higher value to draw off of for income and you did not have to rely on the stock market or the interest rate market to give you gains all those years.

So I use annuities only as an income planning tool within an income plan...not as a growth strategy. I want to find companies that give my clients the highest payout for income with the highest guaranteed rates of return each year on the income value until the client is ready to take it as income. My clients who have owned these types of annuity contracts did not lose one single penny of their money in the stock market meltdowns in 2000, 2001, 2002 or 2008!

The most common objection I always get about annuities is about surrender charges. Let's have a discussion about these surrender charges in annuities. The surrender charge in an annuity is a great thing for the consumer! We have surrender charges wherever we decide to put our money. If you decide to go to your bank and open up a five-year certificate of deposit and then the next day turn around and want that money, there is going to be a surrender charge or surrender penalty for taking that money out early. The same thing can be said if you buy a bond. If you buy a bond and do not wait until the maturity date and the interest rate market does not work in your favor and you get out of the bond early, you could take a loss on the bond. That is an indirect surrender penalty. Furthermore, if you are in the stock market or in a mutual fund and the mutual fund or the stock market heads south and then you need the money, you're taking an indirect surrender charge. They just don't call it a surrender charge, it is referred to as a market loss.

But what if I could tell you that in an annuity, your surrender charge with a good company would typically be anywhere, at a worst-case, around 10% to 15% if you needed all your money back during the first year. Then that surrender charge would decline over a period of years. Let's compare this to the stock market. If I need all my money because of a financial emergency and it's in the stock market and the stock market is down 30% or 40%, then I have just taken a 30% to 40% surrender charge. Again, it's not referred to as a surrender charge, it's a market loss. But it is the same thing, I have less money than what I had in the account before!

So I have no control in the market when it comes to knowing how much I am going to lose when I really need my money. Contrast that with an annuity and even if the surrender charge is 10% or 15%, I know my worst case scenario in that given year. Once again, these surrender charges decline on a year-by-year basis typically. I would much rather know what my worst case scenario is getting out of an investment versus not knowing what my worst-case scenario is going to be because of an unknown market loss.

Also, many of these annuities today will let you out of the annuity early with full balance and no surrender charge penalty if you incur a long term care situation, terminal illness, or death. If you do need money in a given year, most of the companies that offer annuities today will allow you to take out 10% per year of your balance each and every year without penalty.

Remember, the last chapter I talked about using annuities as a 'stage two' income stream in retirement. Stage one income would be a conservative managed account and stage three income would be a longer-term moderate account. The reason why I use the annuities as a centerpiece 'stage two' income stream in the retirement income plan, is because you do not want to turn on the income too quickly in an annuity, due to mortality factors, or you will not get enough income.

So, if you buy one of these annuities with an income rider, like I described above, then you can allow it to continue to gain a certain guaranteed percentage rate of return each year on the income value until you're ready to turn it on for income. This leaves you with a higher income stream later due to the increase in the income value and the increased mortality factor due to age.

I also use annuities in an income plan as a risk counterbalance to the stock market. What I mean by this is that some annuity companies will pay you an upfront bonus on the money that you deposit with them. The bonus can be anywhere between 4% to 10%, depending on the company. It's important to look for an actual value bonus and not just a bonus on the income value. I had one client call me this week to tell me that some person had pitched them an annuity with a 22% bonus! Knowing the companies and the products in the industry, I knew that the 22% was only a bonus on the income value and not the actual value. Also, because the client would have to take the income value out over a period of years, the bonus became really watered down.

What I look for are good annuity companies that offer true upfront bonuses of between 4% and 10% on your money. The bonus can also be used as a stock market counterbalance. For example, if you are down 10% on your stock market accounts... the 10% bonus that you received on your annuity, assuming that you made the same level of investment, would offset that loss. Therefore, on the overall portfolio, you wouldn't be down.

What about annuity company safety? How safe are companies that offer annuities? Again, life insurance companies offer annuities. Every state has to approve the products sold in that state. So there are 50 insurance commissioners approving products for 50 different states. Not all products are approved in all states. The state you buy the product in is what governs which product can be sold. If you move later on and that product was never approved in that state, you're fine. This is because you bought the product in the state that it was approved in.

Everybody always comes into my office and talks about AIG. Let me help educate you about AIG. AIG was not just a life insurance company, AIG was many companies. AIG owned life insurance companies. A couple of these were American General Life Insurance Company and Sun America Life Insurance Company.

Even if AIG had not been bailed out by the federal government, its life insurance companies would have continued to operate and pay claims. This is because those life insurance companies had their own reserves that were greater than dollar for dollar. The problem that AIG had was in its other subsidiary companies, like their mortgage lending division, or their aircraft leasing division.

Even if AIG had gone under and ceased to exist, it would have had no impact on their life insurance companies. In fact, when AIG had to make a decision on which assets they should sell in order to generate money to pay back the government, they were thinking of selling their life insurance operations which were profitable. Luckily, they decided to keep their life insurance operations because those operations were really the only profitable operations of AIG. In fact, after AIG was bailed out by the federal government, its life insurance companies ended up lending AIG money at a lower interest rate than the government. AIG used those monies to pay back the government way ahead of schedule.

But let's say that AIG's life insurance companies had also failed and their reserves had failed. The second line of defense would be other insurance companies buying AIG's life insurance companies books of business. If that did not happen, then the third line of defense is the state guarantee funds. Each state has a state guarantee fund that would also help bail out consumers that owned life insurance contracts or annuity contracts with that particular life insurance company that failed. So there are three backstops or lines of defense when it comes to safety of life insurance companies…reserves, other companies, and state guarantee funds. Compare that to your bank, who only has one line of defense...the FDIC, or compare that to the securities industry who only has SIPC. So insurance companies are very resilient.

Chapter 9

Paying Taxes On Money That You Do Not Use:

Have you ever been in a mutual fund and the mutual fund went down for the year but you still received a tax bill for capital gains or dividends the fund reinvested? What about being in a bank account and having to pay taxes each year on interest that you did not even spend? Does any of this sound familiar?

If you take a look at your federal 1040 tax form, on the very front are two lines that you need to be concerned with. Line 8A is interest that you received for the year from interest-bearing accounts, like bank accounts. Line 9A are ordinary dividends that you received for the year. Both of these lines add back into your ordinary income. Having large amounts on either one of those lines can trigger large taxation on Social Security benefits or an overall higher income tax bracket. The sad thing, is you probably did not even spend this money. You probably had that money…that you now have to claim as income…reinvested back into the mutual fund or the bank account that you're being taxed on.

To give you an example, I recently had a couple come into my office and they owned a large amount of mutual funds. Most of the funds that they owned were outside of an IRA account, so they were in an after-tax brokerage account. After looking at their tax return I almost dropped out of my chair. They paid over $70,000 more last year in federal and state income taxes because of a large amount of dividend income on line 9A and also a large amount of capital gains distributions, line 13, of the 1040 tax form. I then looked further into the return and noticed that they are also subject to alternative minimum tax, or AMT.

So what would a simple solution be to remove a lot of that income off of the return? If a lot of that after tax mutual fund money was in annuities, then they would not have to pay that $70,000 extra income tax. Annuities grow tax-deferred if they are outside of an IRA. So the money that they did earn, could've been reinvested inside the annuity without any tax effect until they decided to pull it out. I have no problem paying income tax on money that I spend and use. But, I do have a problem paying tax on money that I don't spend and that I don't use.

This is one simple strategy of how buying annuities in an after tax account can help you with income taxes you have to pay on an annual basis. The annuity can reduce or eliminate a lot of the tax on money you paid taxes on but did not spend. Inside of an IRA account, there is no tax advantage to owning an annuity because you are already tax-deferred. Then it becomes all about using the right kind of annuities to protect against stock market loss and also generate guaranteed lifetime income. So, it's not just about the tax deferral for annuities, it also becomes a factor of guaranteed growth for future income needs and preservation of principal against stock market loss for any annuities you would put inside of an IRA account.

Annuities are also not subject to AMT, or alternative minimum tax calculations. Tax free municipal bonds are still subject to AMT and their tax free income can also affect Social Security threshold income for Social Security tax calculation purposes. The income from tax free municipal bonds gets added back in as 'threshold income' to determine what percentage of your social security is subject to taxation. Their income also factors into the AMT calculation. So they're not truly 'tax free'. Tax deferred annuities outside of an IRA account are not subject to any of this. So annuities can also really help with reducing income tax and AMT on an overall tax return.

Chapter 10

The Importance of Long Term Care Planning:

Long term care can be devastating to loved ones and to the pocketbook of the person receiving care. I have first-hand experience with long term care. My grandmother was in long term care for over 12 years. Her transition was from a senior living apartment to assisted living facilities and then to full-blown nursing home care. When she was in her early 80s she fell and broke her hip. Up until that time she had been living mostly independently, but had been in and out of assisted living facilities. But the hip break was the final straw. This is what sent her into long term convalescent care.

As a person who had Parkinson's disease for over 40 years, my grandmother was unable to work in the regular workforce. She relied on Social Security disability and then Social Security for her income. She relied on California's Medi-Cal program (California's version of Medicaid) to pay for her long term care needs. The facilities that she had to endure and live in, I would not want to wish on my worst enemy. She did not have the luxury of homecare because Medicare typically does not pay for homecare and Medi-Cal normally only pays for homecare in extreme circumstances. Since she had no money and no assets her only choice was to go into facility care.

The clients that I deal with typically have a good deal of money that they have saved for retirement and many own a home. In their case, Medicare and Medi-Cal would not pay much, if anything, for their long term care needs. They would need to spend down nearly all of their assets in order to get long term care covered by Medi-Cal. Medicare only covers 100 days lifetime of long term care and then that is it.

So it is critical to have a long term care strategy in place. The problem with long term care insurance today is that over the years it has been an underpriced product. You see, once insurance companies first started to sell long term care policies about 20 years ago, they thought the average age of the person buying the policy would be about 45 years old. It turned out that the average purchaser of long term care insurance is well into their 60s. Therefore, the life insurance companies that sell this product, or sold this product, did not have enough time to allow the money that they took in from premiums to reinvest and grow in order to pay the claims.

What has happened over the years is that many companies have pulled out of various states and the companies that have stayed have increased premiums substantially. The companies that have left a particular state have also many times increased premium at a very high rate. A couple came to me about three years ago and showed me a letter that they had received from their insurance company showing that there would be a 90% rate increase over a two-year period on their long term care insurance. That carrier is still in business, but left the state and is no longer writing policies in California. The clients had two options, either pay the increased premium or reduce the benefit.

For them, myself, my mother and many of my other clients, I transitioned them to something called asset-based long term care insurance. With asset-based long term care insurance, think about it like a partnership between you and the life insurance company. For a couple of years, you are responsible for the long term care payments should you need to go into long term care. But after that two years, then the life insurance company could be on the hook for the rest of your life depending on options selected within the product.

The money that you paid into that first couple of years of care sits in essentially a low paying savings account until you're ready to use the money for long term care. If you never use the money for long term care, it grows at an interest rate and then you have a guaranteed amount coming back to you at any certain year should you decide to cancel the policy. If you die, and never use the money for long term care, your beneficiaries get a higher benefit than your original lump sum premium that you put in.

So asset-based long term care can be a pretty good solution for people who still want to have long term care insurance but don't want to have rate increases, or lose money that they paid into premiums should they never use it.

Chapter 11

You Mean I Get Taxed At Death Too?

I always get an occasional couple who comes into my office and thinks that because they have a living trust in place, their beneficiaries are never going to have to pay income taxes at their deaths. Wrong!

First, let's discuss probably the largest investment that you have besides your house. That investment is probably a 401(k) or an IRA. At your death or your spouse's death, a non-spouse beneficiary will have to pay income tax on those accounts. If your spouse is the primary beneficiary of your IRA or 401(k), they can rollover the account into an IRA for themselves at your death and there will not be any income tax on the rollover. However the surviving spouse will still be subject to required minimum distribution when they reach age 70 1/2 years old. Once they die, and the IRA transfers to non-spouse beneficiaries, then the whole amount becomes taxable...unless certain tax 'stretch' options are elected.

If your beneficiaries elect to stretch the IRA proceeds over their lifetime, they can continue to grow the IRA in a tax-deferred state, but will have to take out a required minimum distribution each year called a beneficiary distribution. On the surface, this may sound like an excellent option. But in reality, the beneficiary will pay more in income taxes to the IRS over their life expectancy then if they were just to take the IRA lump sum at the last spouse's death and pay the income tax.

Where this 'stretch' option can work very well is within an inherited Roth IRA account. In that case, the non-spouse beneficiary can stretch the nontaxable Roth IRA account over their life expectancy and grow the account tax-free, distribute the account tax-free and it will always be tax-free money. The beneficiary still has to take a required distribution every year out of the inherited Roth IRA account but it will never be taxed. Leaving this type of an account to your beneficiaries instead of a fully taxable IRA account can be a legacy that your beneficiaries will always appreciate and remember you for the rest of their lives. Think about each year that they get the tax-free distribution check that they have to take and they remember that it was you that left that for them!

However, the only person who can rollover a regular IRA account to a Roth IRA account is the original owner of the IRA account or the original owner's spouse. Once the money gets to the non-spouse beneficiaries, if it is still a regular IRA, the beneficiary cannot rollover that IRA account to a Roth IRA account. This is because inherited IRA accounts have different rules then non-inherited IRA accounts. The best way to leave your kids or non-spouse beneficiaries money is to leave them tax free money! They will always remember and appreciate you for leaving them a tax free legacy!

So then, when is the best time to roll over your existing IRA or 401(k) account to a Roth IRA account? The best time to do this is at the death of the first spouse. The surviving spouse should then roll over the existing fully taxable IRA account to a tax-free Roth IRA account. That way, the surviving spouse can leave the Roth IRA account to non-spouse beneficiaries and they can take it as an inherited Roth IRA account and stretch all of the tax free tax benefit over their life expectancy!

But what about the tax that will be generated once the surviving spouse rolls over the existing IRA to a Roth IRA? How does that tax get paid? Taxes on a large IRA account could be anywhere between

30% and 50% depending on the state you live in and the federal and state income tax rates that you are at. The best solution for this is to buy what I call 'tax insurance'.

What is tax insurance? Tax insurance is simply life insurance. You buy a life insurance policy and make your spouse the primary beneficiary and your children or non-spouse beneficiaries the contingent beneficiary. Now I know what you're saying, "Mark I do not need life insurance. I have enough money and don't need any kind of income replacement". To that, I would say you are absolutely correct... you do not need life insurance. What you do need is tax insurance.

You see, the government is going to take away 30% to 50% of what you saved in your IRA plan should you die and not have that already rolled over to Roth IRA. You're going to pay taxes either now or later. So why not take the money that you will be paying in taxes over your lifetime on your IRA accounts now and channel some of that to a tax free life insurance policy that will act as a tax insurance backstop for your loved ones?

The ideal situation is to put the life insurance on both spouses' lives, not just one spouse, because you don't know who is going to die first. However, sometimes only one spouse can qualify and that is the best solution. Half a loaf is better than no loaf at all. Life insurance proceeds are all tax free from income tax. Therefore they are a great source of funds to pay the tax bill once the surviving spouse completes the Roth IRA rollover. Once that conversion happens, the surviving spouse never ever has to take a required distribution again. Roth IRA's are not subject to minimum required distribution age 70 1/2 rules.

Let's talk about a second need for tax insurance. Today, if you are married and your overall estate is under $10.9 million (2016 exemptions) at the death of the 2nd spouse, then there is no estate tax or 'death tax' owed. But if your estate is over that amount, at the second spouse's death, estate taxes will be owed on the overage. So let's talk about the things that add into the estate tax equation. Aside from standard investments and real estate, the other things that can add into the estate tax equation are qualified accounts like 401(k)s and IRA accounts and also life insurance!

If you have a large estate near the exemption limit or in excess of that amount, the life insurance should be put into something called a 'life insurance trust' outside of the estate. If you are near or at the federal estate tax exemption limit, the life insurance inside the estate could be more damaging than not having it at all, since it is included in the federal estate tax calculation if it is owned by you and not a life insurance trust. So a properly designed estate plan needs to be put into place.

Also, the qualified accounts, like your IRA or 401(k), could be double taxed in a situation where you are above the estate tax maximum exemption limit. At the death of the last spouse, not only would your heirs have to pay ordinary income tax on the amount of money in your IRAs or 401(k) accounts, they would also have to pay estate tax (death tax) on that money as well!

Let me use an example of what I am talking about when it comes to double taxation of assets. A short while ago there was a $1.5 billion Powerball lottery jackpot. If there had been only one winner, that winner would've received a $900 million lump sum if they chose that option! But, by the time the income taxes were paid on that $900 million, there would only be about $550 million left over for that winner. Let's say that the winner died the very next day after claiming the jackpot and paying the income taxes. Now the beneficiaries, who would receive the $550 million from the deceased winner, would have to pay estate tax also on that $550 million! It's a double whammy! This is why tax insurance is so important. A properly designed estate plan, including tax insurance outside of the estate, could be used to pay all of that tax so that the heirs are made whole.

So tax planning becomes very important, not just during your lifetime but also at death...to make sure that the government does not get the bulk of what you worked so hard for.

Chapter 12

Pension Replacement, How Will You Continue to Live On Less?

If you are working with an advisor right now or a stockbroker, have they ever asked you what happens to your spouse's pension when they pass away? Did they ever ask how much the surviving spouse gets or whether or not the surviving spouse will get anything at all?

Pension replacement planning is critical today because depending the way that you took your pension, your surviving spouse may get half or nothing at all when you die. Also, pension planning is critical if you have not yet selected a benefit and are due a pension when you retire. Making the wrong pension election can be damaging and irreversible.

The other consideration with regards to a decreased income at the death of a spouse is Social Security benefits. The surviving spouse will typically get the larger of either their benefit or the deceased spouse's benefit. But, the surviving spouse does not get to keep both benefits. Therefore, there would be an additional loss of income because of the death of a spouse.

Make sure you take these things into consideration when designing your overall retirement income plan and understand alternatives when it comes to selecting the correct pension option.

Chapter 13

The Retirement Income Wheel™:

A while back I came up with a strategy to illustrate the way a proper retirement income plan should be designed. Retirement can be very confusing and I thought that this Retirement Income Wheel™ explanation would simply illustrate all the elements required within a properly designed lifetime income plan.

I call it the Retirement Income Wheel™, because I want you to think of traveling down the road through retirement. However, if you do not have all the spokes in your wheel operating properly, your wheel will collapse and you will not make it all the way down the retirement income road.

On the next page you will see my Retirement Income Wheel™. There are four spokes in the wheel. Each spoke represents a necessary component to make sure that you survive retirement.

Retirement Income Wheel ™

PROTECTION
(TAX INS.)
(LTC.)

GUARANTEED ②
LIFETIME
INCOME *
(ANNUITY SOLUTIONS)

MODERATE
MANAGED
5 to 7+ years
before
we use this
spoke!
③

CONSERVATIVE ①
MANAGED
DIVIDENDS
↓ YIELD

*Guaranteed by
the claims paying
ability of the
Insurance Company

TURN ON → 1, 2, 3

81

From left to right, the first spoke is the protection spoke. In the protection spoke is where we have things like long term care planning and tax insurance. The next spoke is the guaranteed income spoke, so that you have lifetime income. This spoke is typically designed with fixed indexed annuities with an income rider, as I detailed in a previous chapter. The next spoke is a conservative income account. This spoke is designed with income producing managed accounts, accounts that pay out stock dividends and also bond income. To decrease volatility, there is a larger concentration of bonds in that managed account than stock. The goal is to use this money without having large losses of value. The last spoke is a moderate managed account. With this spoke, you can potentially lose a lot of money but also make a lot of money. But remember, this spoke is the last spoke that you would get into when you need income.

Now, let's discuss staging your income from the Retirement Income Wheel™. The first stage of income would be the conservative managed account spoke. The reason for this is because it is low in volatility and also offers income being paid out instead of just relying on returns of the stock market. The income is generated through both bond yield and stock dividends. As you are spending down this spoke, which is anticipated, we are building up the other two spokes because you do not yet need them for income. Typically, I like to channel about 35% of your investments to this conservative spoke.

The second stage of income would be from the annuities spoke. You do not want to use this as a first stage of income because the annuities have not had long enough to grow with their guaranteed income rider percentages and you are not yet old enough, due to mortality factors, to receive a lot of income out of those products if you turn them on right away. So you will want to wait a few years before you invade the annuities for income. This is why I staged them as a stage two income strategy within the Retirement Income Wheel™. Typically, I like to channel approximately 50% of your investments to this guaranteed income spoke.

Finally, the third stage of retirement income would come from the moderate managed account spoke. It is likely that this stage is more than 10 years out and therefore you do not really have to worry about the ups and downs of the market during that time frame. Typically, I like to channel 15% of your investments to this spoke.

If you look at risk in the plan, since 85% of your investible money is in the conservative or guaranteed income spokes, much of the loss potential and volatility on your portfolio has been eliminated. The 15% that typically goes into the moderate spoke, may have a large decrease in value but not much relative to the overall portfolio. For example, if someone had a $1 million portfolio, there would only be 15% or $150,000 that would be in the moderate spoke. Instead of losing 30% of $1 million, or $300k, in a severe market correction (if you were mostly into a moderate investment style before our remodel), your loss on the moderate account would now be only $45k, if your moderate account corrected 30%. This means out of an entire $1 million portfolio, the moderate piece has only caused a total loss of 4.5% on the entire portfolio. This is much more palatable than a minus 30% on the entire portfolio. Even if you had a 10% additional slip on the conservative accounts, the bonuses on the annuity spoke would cover all the losses plus more in this case.

So the Retirement Income Wheel™ is a critical and powerful planning strategy within an overall retirement income plan.

Chapter 14

The Smart Sleeves Income Plan™:

Finally, I take all of the accounts that we have created with the Retirement Income Wheel™ and I then fit those into the Smart Sleeves Income Plan™ that has been dictated by the budget that you provided at the onset of our journey.

What is the Smart Sleeves Income Plan™? The Smart Sleeves Income Plan™ is an income staging strategy that will show you when and for how long you need to take money out of the conservative, guaranteed income, and moderate spokes of the Retirement Income Wheel™.

Using the budget that you provided at the onset, the Smart Sleeves Income Plan™ closes the retirement income gap that we talked about in earlier chapters. The retirement income gap is an income shortfall that you still need to makeup from your investments after all sources of income from Social Security, pensions, and other income has been accounted for.

You can see in the next illustration, a sample portion of a Smart Sleeves Income Plan™. The conservative managed account is used first, then the guaranteed income annuity, and then finally the moderate managed account.

Using an income staging method like this during retirement allows you to fulfill your income needs without jeopardizing all of your assets to market risk or invading each account each year because you need to take out money to live off of.

(See Smart Sleeves Income Plan™ illustration next page)

Smart Sleeves Income Plan™

Planning Horizon 40 / hypothetical	Him	Her	Trust - Conservative Managed		Trust - F Squared Sector Rotation Mgd		NQ - Annuity #1			NQ - Annuity #2		
Year	Him	Her	Account	Income	Account	Income	Account	Inc Rider	Income	Account	Inc Rider	Income
net return	66	67	5.55%	make up	8.00%	make up	2.00%	7.00%	jt rider	2.00%	7.00%	jt rider
investment			890,152		260,000		249,252	SIA 7%		249,252	SIA 7%	
bonus %			0.0%		0.0%		7.0%	7.0%		7.0%	7.0%	
w/bonus			890,152		260,000		266,700	266,700		266,700	266,700	
end of 1	67	68	878,090	61,465	280,800	0	272,034	285,369	0	272,034	285,369	0
end of 2	68	69	848,653	78,171	303,264		277,474	305,344		277,474	305,344	
end of 3	69	70	809,394	86,360	327,525		283,024	326,719		283,024	326,719	
end of 4	70	71	769,721	84,594	353,727		288,684	349,589		288,684	349,589	
end of 5	71	72	759,361	53,079	382,025		294,458	374,060		294,458	374,060	
end of 6	72	73	742,863	58,643	412,587		300,347	400,244		300,347	400,244	
end of 7	73	74	742,527	43,564	445,594		283,540		22,814	306,354	428,261	
end of 8	74	75	736,264	47,475	481,242		266,397		22,814	312,461	458,240	
end of 9	75	76	750,601	26,526	519,741		248,911		22,814	291,695		27,036
end of 10	76	77	759,458	32,801	561,320		231,075		22,814	270,492		27,036
end of 11	77	78	737,140	64,468	606,226		212,883		22,814	248,866		27,036
end of 12	78	79	706,919	71,133	654,724		194,327		22,814	226,807		27,036
end of 13	79	80	668,152	78,001	707,102		175,399		22,814	204,307		27,036
end of 14	80	81	620,154	85,080	763,670		156,093		22,814	181,357		27,036
end of 15	81	82	595,821	58,752	824,764		136,401		22,814	157,948		27,036
end of 16	82	83	563,627	65,262	890,745		116,315		22,814	134,071		27,036
end of 17	83	84	522,935	71,973	962,005		95,828		22,814	109,716		27,036
end of 18	84	85	473,067	78,891	1,038,965		74,930		22,814	84,875		27,036
end of 19	85	86	413,300	86,022	1,122,082		53,615		22,814	59,536		27,036
end of 20	86	87	342,865	93,375	1,211,849		31,873		22,814	33,651		27,036
end of 21	87	88	260,943	100,951	1,308,797		9,697		22,814	7,328		27,036
end of 22	88	89	166,663	108,763	1,413,501		0		22,814	0		27,036
end of 23	89	90	59,097	116,816	1,526,581		0		22,814	0		27,036
end of 24	90	91	0	62,376	1,585,964	62,743	0		22,814	0		27,036
end of 25	91	92	1		1,579,162	133,679	0		22,814	0		27,036
end of 26	92	93	1		1,562,990	142,505	0		22,814	0		27,036
end of 27	93	94	1		1,536,425	151,604	0		22,814	0		27,036
end of 28	94	95	1		1,496,353	160,986	0		22,814	0		27,036
end of 29	95	96	1		1,447,563	170,659	0		22,814	0		27,036
end of 30	96	97	1		1,382,734	180,634	0		22,814	0		27,036
end of 31	97	98	1		1,302,433	190,919	0		22,814	0		27,036
end of 32	98	99	1		1,205,104	201,524	0		22,814	0		27,036
end of 33	99	100	1		1,089,051	212,461	0		22,814	0		27,036
end of 34	100	101	1		952,437	223,799	0		22,814	0		27,036

Conservative style buckets carry this client through the first 24 yrs of the plan. The moderate bucket doesn't need to be accessed until year 24. The annuities provide lifetime income years 7+

Chapter 15

The Next Step to Your Retirement Security:

As I wind down this book, I hope that it has brought you a lot of insight that maybe you did not have prior to reading it. My goal is not to compete with your current advisor or you, if you are trading or managing your own accounts, but instead to offer you a solution in retirement that can allow you to live the rest of your retirement years without having to worry about whether or not you will be able to survive.

If you would like to find out more information about some of these planning strategies, I invite you to reach out to my office to set up a 15 minute Retirement Income Checkup call with me over the telephone to see if you would be a candidate for my kind of work. If after the Retirement Income Checkup telephone assessment, we both mutually feel that you could benefit from my planning strategies, then I will invite you to my office in Calabasas, California for an in-depth review of everything that you have and I will perform further analysis and make further recommendations based upon your unique needs and circumstances.

The next page offers you contact information for me and also how you can take advantage of my complementary Retirement Income Checkup telephone assessment.

I am here for you if you need my help…but you have to want my help. I can only help those who truly want the help.

Thank you again for your time and attention and I look forward to hearing from you at some point in the future of you would like help. If you feel a friend could benefit from this book and if they are in or nearing retirement, please pass this onto them and have them call my office for a complementary Retirement Income Checkup telephone assessment.

How to Contact Mark Kennedy

➢ To receive your complimentary Retirement Income Checkup, visit the website at:
www.retirementincomecheckup.com

➢ To inquire about upcoming workshops, please call the office toll free at **(888) 805-1541** during normal business hours 9am-5pm Pacific Time, Monday thru Friday.

➢ If you would like Mark to speak for your company, church, synagogue, group or organization, please call the office toll free at **(888) 805-1541** during normal business hours 9am-5pm Pacific Time, Monday thru Friday.

➢ If you would like to schedule a face-to-face or phone meeting with Mark, please call the office toll free at **(888) 805-1541** during normal business hours 9am-5pm Pacific Time, Monday thru Friday.